VICTORIA
MEKHI BUFO
with Dr. Nic

Breaking
JARS

THE STORY OF FLEAS
& LEARNED HELPLESSNESS

VICTORIA ROLLINS
DR. NICOLE PRICE
with Mekhi Buford-Page

Breaking
JARS

THE STORY OF FLEAS
& LEARNED HELPLESSNESS

Content and cover imagery:
Mekhi Buford Page, Dr. Nicole Price, and
Victoria Rollins

Hand drawn imagery: Deaunte Thomas

Breaking Jars: The Story of Fleas and Learned
Helplessness

ISBN: 9798399310978
Imprint: Independently published

The Flea Story

Once upon a time, there were fleas who lived in a big, clear jar. They jumped, but never too high. The fleas didn't seem to know why, but that's what their parents and grandparents did, and so they did too.

One day a flea asked, "Do you ever wonder why we never jump out of this space? Even when other fleas jump really high, we don't seem to be able to leap out." it said.

"It's not something other fleas were taught to think about. But us fleas? We stay inside—confined."

Then an elder flea began to speak. "Long ago we had never seen jars and we jumped freely."

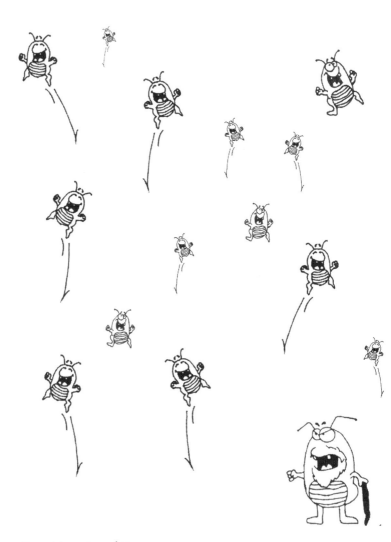

"Dog scientists put us in a large jar. At first, we were in the jar, but without a lid. We have never had wings, but we were able to jump almost 100 times our body length in distance, so we all jumped out."

"Then the scientist put a lid on the jar!" He shouted.
"We jumped and jumped."

"Some of us jumped so hard we hurt ourselves. Once we realized we couldn't jump any higher, we learned not to try. Even after the lid was gone, we still jumped low."

Grandpa began with, "Let me tell you a specific story about how we came to know the dog scientists, how Fajardo, Lola, Adam, and Sage got swindled, and ultimately, how we all got tricked."

"Once upon a time, there was a flea named Eddie who wanted to explore the world," Grandpa started.

"His friends, Fajardo, Lola, Adam, and Sage, didn't like his idea. They believed in finding a host and living a long, healthy life as true parasites. They tried to convince Eddie to live a 'regular life,' hoping he would change his mind."

"He understood their point but didn't want to settle for something ordinary. He wanted to push himself, take risks, and see what he was capable of."

The regular flea life might be safe," Eddie sighed, "but it's also predictable and limited."

Eddie thought his friends could be right. Later that day, Eddie discovered a mysterious laboratory and met a scientist named Dr. Malus. The scientist promised Eddie a normal flea life, full of stability, security, and everything he desired. Eddie was tempted by this offer and ran to share the news with his friends.

He told his friends about Dr. Malus' offer,
they were unsure about trusting the
scientist. They worried about his motives
and whether he could really give them a
normal flea life.

Eddie assured his friends that Dr. Malus genuinely wanted to help them. He convinced them to give it a chance and agreed to introduce them to the scientist.

The fleas started walking to the laboratory all of them hesitating but Eddie. Upon arrival Mr.Malus meets them at the entrance. Once Eddie and his friends entered the laboratory, they realized that something was not right. Dr. Malus, the scientist, had tricked them. The promises of a normal flea life turned out to be false.

Inside the jar where they were trapped, there was no food or water. The space was small and uncomfortable. Eddie felt guilty for leading his friends into this situation, but he refused to give up.

Days turned into a week, and hope started to fade. But just when they thought all was lost, but Dr. Malus had removed the lid and Eddie tried to convince them but Sage, Adam and Lola didn't see a point in trying. Fajardo was planning to leave so she joined Eddie and decided to leave, too.

Eddie told Fajardo

"we may have lost some of our friends,
but we mustn't let their despair
overshadow our own spark of hope. Let's
support one another and keep searching
for a way out because I don't do jars. We
owe it to ourselves to try. I don't know
why they would want to stay in a jar
anyways weirdos."

Upset, Grandpa ended his story there.

This is how we got tricked. Today, every story is about what's wrong with us fleas and hardly a soul talks about Dr. Malus.

"Now, it's what we know. We even hold the trauma in our bodies."

The young fleas spoke up, "That doesn't sound fair.

Maybe it's time for us to jump for the skies again, and maybe," they hesitated, "just maybe, it's time to teach those scientists a thing or two about us fleas."

And so, the young fleas wrote a letter to the scientists. They asked for the scientists to be honest about the jars and lids. They also demanded justice for their ancestors who were subjected to those jars and lids. They stated that if the damage was repaired, truth, healing, and reconciliation could begin.

The scientist, Dr. Malus, was surprised by their actions. When he first got the letter, he was a bit smug about it.

"Well, it seems our little friends have more spirit than we thought. Perhaps we have underestimated them."

The letter stated the injustices of the jars and the lids. The fleas expressed that they did not deserve to be part of an experiment. They wondered if the scientists would have done something like this to members of their own families.

The scientists listened and began to understand.

They saw that their experiment had consequences. But the fleas wanted more than just an apology; they wanted things to change.

The scientists, realizing their mistakes, decided to make amends.

They provided the fleas with resources: soft moss for comfort, tiny shelters for protection, and food to keep them strong.

A different, bold flea with lots of courage started to speak. "We appreciate your efforts, but remember, reparations are just a start." the flea said.

"We still need assurance this won't happen again, and that others learn from this too."

Dr. Malus said, "You're right, we were wrong. We'll work to make amends, and we will remember your story, so this never happens again."

The scientists continued to take responsibility for their actions, and worked to fix things.

Dr. Greenfield, another scientist, continued to talk with the fleas.

He traveled the world talking educating anyone who would listen.

"This is to help support our global community and make up for the difficulties we've caused."

The second flea jumped for joy. "Look at us now! We can jump high again, we can leap far. We're not just an experiment. We're fleas with a spirit that soars beyond this jar!"

From then on, the fleas were never put in a jar again.

They jumped as high as they wanted, reminding everyone, big or small, to fight for harm to be repaired and never let a lid limit their stifle your beliefs about what is possible.

And you, dear reader, remember this:
when you see a lid on someone's dreams,
help them take it off.

Break jars and repair harm.

Let's ensure everyone can reach their
own sky, just like our brave little fleas.

Exploring the Concept

Consider this:

What if the 'fleas' from our story don't only represent the typical communities we have come to label as minority, marginalized, and underrepresented, but also represent those who hold power?

Just as the fleas learned to limit their jumps because of the lid placed over them, could it be that the ones in power have also developed their own form of learned helplessness?

In this case, the jar represents the system within which power brokers operate.

The lid symbolizes the self-imposed constraints and limiting beliefs, often resulting from the fear of challenging the status quo, going against the grain, or upsetting the balance.

Just as the fleas were conditioned to believe that they could not jump any higher than the lid, the people in power are often conditioned to believe that they cannot change the system, that it is too rigid or too complex to be reformed.

But what if the lid was taken off? What if the people in power realized that they, too, were under the influence of their own learned helplessness, entrapped within an invisible barrier, bounded by their preconceived beliefs and fears?

What if they saw that they have the ability to challenge, to change, and to dismantle the oppressive systems that they have unknowingly reinforced?

When the fleas realized that the jar was open, they found their true potential to leap high, unbounded by the confines of the jar. Similarly, when power brokers realize the boundaries they perceive are self-imposed, they might discover their ability to implement change is far greater than they thought.

They hold the power to enact significant, transformative policies and practices that can actively dismantle the oppressive systems at play.

But here's the crux: acknowledging the existence of the invisible lid is the first, most important step. Only then can those in power begin to challenge their own limiting beliefs, thus catalyzing the reformation of systems that have long been accepted as 'just the way things are.'

So, we ask you to contemplate this: Are you, perhaps, a flea in your own jar?

And more importantly, are you ready to recognize your jar for what it is and leap beyond its invisible confines?

"The problem in the world is the oppression of man by man; it is this which threatens existence."
—Lorraine Hansberry

Real World Relatability

Let's think about rich people as the person in power and people without homes as the ones without power.

When we ask rich people to help those without money, many feel that by giving their money away they're losing something.

The reality is, that the richest 1% of people often have multiple sources of income. When they give, they have the luxury of making even more money while they sleep in interest. Still, they get frustrated at the idea of losing.

They tend to put forth less effort towards solving the problem. Many donate to outside organizations instead of investing directly into the community around them. Charity becomes safer than justice. This is just one way that symptoms of learned helplessness might show up for people in power.

"Charity feels safer than justice."

—Dr. Nicole Price

Signs of
Learned Helplessness

Saying things like: "It's out of my hands" or "If I do that, I'm putting myself at risk"

Frustration

Giving up

 Lack of effort despite encouragement

Why would people in power avoid aiding those who have little power?

When these people in power use the power they hold for harm or gain, they aren't considering themselves as part of a global community. They obviously aren't considering others. Is this because they believe harm done to others does not come back on them?

When you learn to be helpless, you forget that you have the ability to do something. Unfortunately, when people hear the flea story, they start to think the fleas are people without power.

Learned helplessness is the study of human behavior. It is not the study of the behavior of people living in poverty, or people without houses, or any other specific group.

As such, people WITH power suffer from learned helplessness, too. The fleas represent the thoughts of the people in power in our world. Their thinking is trapped in the idea that we do not have enough for everyone to go around.

What about you?

Do you have power? Whatever your answer, are you sure? We've seen children wield power over other children and even animals.

Favored children use the power of parental favor for evil at times.

Do you have a home? Are you nasty to people who live on the streets?

It is important to think about your power positions so that you can behave differently. Without reflection, it seems like it's worth placing fleas in jars because leaders have been learning for decades the effects of learned helplessness.

But is anyone asking about the fleas?

Now, if the fleas are people, then the scientists are the actual ones in power, like maybe leaders in governments, or school systems. The lid is like the rules or conditions that keep people from reaching their full potential. These people in power are putting their minds in this limiting jar, and creating problems for themselves that don't even exist.

The scientists are *wrong* frfr*!

*for real, for real

Power can be gained in many different forms.

Power can be:
- Politics
- Money
- People trusting your words

When you have power in some part of life that other people don't, you become scared to lose it.

People in power create these "jars" to feel safe in the new power they've been given. They use the lids as a way to box others in and defend their actions by overly focusing on the behaviors of others.

In other words, if I feel like I can't help you without hurting myself, I won't help you.

They teach themselves to not be able to help, to protect their power.

Let's scale it down a bit,
shall we?

Another example could be a boss at work.

This person has huge amounts of power over the people who report to them.

Every decision they make affects the employees.

Bosses usually have to check in with their own boss, depending on how high up the ladder they are in that company.

If the employees at a company have a problem, and the boss can't fix it, they have to go to the person in power to change it. Sometimes, when the issue doesn't seem big enough or the boss has tried to change it, they stop trying. This becomes learned helplessness. They don't think they can change things for the employees. They become less persistent and slow down on attempts at change.

Identifying

&

Categorizing

Recognizing signs and
how to deal with them.

Identifying

jars

and

lids

Recognizing Discriminatory Behavior of People in Power

When people in power act unfairly or treat others differently because of who they are, it's called discriminatory behavior. Sometimes, they don't even realize they're doing it. They might make choices that favor some people while leaving others behind. This can make the people who are already having a hard time feel even worse.

Judging Those in the Jar

Sometimes, people in power look down on those who don't have power. They might think that those people are not as important or capable as they are. They don't think about the challenges others face or try to understand their point of view. This can make it harder for them to help, or make things better for everyone. They may judge and make assumptions about individuals or groups without considering other factors that contribute to their circumstances. This judgment can lead to a lack of empathy and understanding of the challenges faced by those in underrepresented positions.

A Single Story

People in power may adopt a narrow and limited perspective, focusing only on their own experiences and interests. They don't think about how others might feel or what they might be going through, particularly those without power. This can make it difficult for them to understand the problems that others face and to make fair decisions that help everyone.

Lack of Individual Accountability

People in power don't always take responsibility for their actions or the impact they have on others. They might blame others or say it's not their fault when things go wrong. This can make it hard to make things better and to fix the problems that exist. In the case of the story, the doctor wanting to focus on the money instead of ways to help people and fleas was the lack of accountability.

Assumptions

Sometimes, people in power make assumptions about others based on their own experiences or what they've seen happen to a few individuals. They might think that everyone who is struggling is lazy or doesn't want to do better. They don't realize that everyone's situation is different and that there are bigger reasons why some people are having a hard time.

In some cases, a chosen person or group may be selected out of a group of underrepresented people. This could be used to make people without power feel better about having a little bit of representation. It distracts from the jar and the lid, by giving them a visual of people of made it out of the jar.

In this story, "jars" are like the systems or rules that keep people trapped and make it hard for them to succeed.

These systems can include social, economic, political, or cultural practices that help keep the power uneven.

"Lids" are like the beliefs or attitudes that people in power have that keep things the same and stop them from changing. These systems and beliefs are not fair and make it harder for everyone to have a fair chance.

Breaking

jars

and

removing lids

Jars and lids are not automatically positive or negative. While they can be progressive, or potentially toxic, jars and lids are tools. It is the people who utilize and monitor the tools that set the stage for how things work.

Jars and lids can be made by people in power, but they can also be changed. It's important for people in power to understand the impact of their choices and to work towards making things better.

We all have power in some ways. We also have the power to break down the unfair systems. This is especially true when we are in powerful positions and have resources. We can challenge our own beliefs to create a more equal and just society where everyone has a chance to succeed.

"People can collectively generate the kind of power that can be earth shaking...bring the kind of pressure that causes us to imagine a future without war and without racism and without prisons."

—Angela Davis

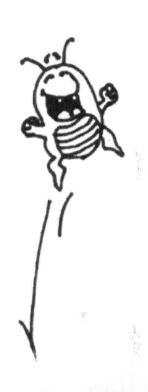

"Cultural patterns of oppression are not only interrelated but are bound together and influenced by the intersectional systems of society. Examples of this include race, gender, class, ability, and ethnicity."

—Kimberle Williams Crenshaw

What are thoughts that came up for you while you read this book?

_____

_____

_____

_____

_____

_____

_____

_____

_____

_____

Who do the fleas represent in our society? Can they represent different groups or individuals depending on the perspective?

In what ways are the scientists' actions similar to those of people in positions of power today?

_____

_____

_____

_____

_____

_____

_____

_____

_____

_____

How could the concept of "learned helplessness" apply to both the fleas and the scientists? Can you identify examples of learned helplessness in your own life or in society?

_____

_____

_____

_____

_____

_____

_____

_____

_____

_____

How do the reparations provided by the scientists help the fleas? What do these reparations symbolize in the context of our society?

_____

_____

_____

_____

_____

_____

_____

_____

_____

_____

In the story, what does the act of the fleas writing a letter to the scientists represent? How does this relate to real-world actions taken by marginalized groups?

How did the narrative change when the perspective shifted to consider the people in power as the 'fleas'? How does this alter the way you think about power dynamics and responsibility in society?

What can we learn from the fleas and apply to our own lives or communities in order to create positive change?

What are some ways that individuals with power can challenge their own learned helplessness and take action towards dismantling oppressive systems?

What are some ways that individuals with power can challenge their own learned helplessness and take action towards dismantling oppressive systems?

_____

_____

_____

_____

_____

_____

_____

_____

_____

_____

What is the key message you have taken from this story, and how will it influence your actions moving forward?

_____

_____

_____

_____

_____

_____

_____

_____

_____

_____

Printed in Great Britain
by Amazon